He was born in Trinidad, West Indies, in 1955. Son of a journalist, came to UK in 1961 with mother, siblings and grandmother. Went to Keele University in 1973. Left in 1975. Returned to London University in 1989. Graduated in philosophy in 1993. Published the *End of Existence* in 1998. This went into three editions.

Thinker and Friend, for inspiration and clarification of ideas.

Leon Lorenzo Leslie

I will not cease from mental fight,
Nor shall my sword sleep in my hand,
'Til we have built Jerusalem,
In England's green and pleasant land.

Garvin Rampersad

Mental Fight

Austin Macauley Publishers

LONDON · CAMBRIDGE · NEW YORK · SHARJAH

Copyright © Garvin Rampersad 2023

The right of Garvin Rampersad to be identified as author of this work has been asserted by the author in accordance with sections 77 and 78 of the Copyright, Designs and Patents Act 1988.

All rights reserved. No part of this publication may be reproduced, stored in a retrieval system, or transmitted in any form or by any means, electronic, mechanical, photocopying, recording, or otherwise, without the prior permission of the publishers.

Any person who commits any unauthorised act in relation to this publication may be liable to criminal prosecution and civil claims for damages.

A CIP catalogue record for this title is available from the British Library.

ISBN 9781528955720 (Paperback)
ISBN 9781528956925 (Hardback)
ISBN 9781528957601 (ePub e-book)
ISBN 9781528957571 (Audiobook)

www.austinmacauley.com

First Published 2023
Austin Macauley Publishers Ltd®
1 Canada Square
Canary Wharf
London
E14 5AA

Professor Fiona Ellis, Professor Sir Roger Scruton and David Wiggins.

Foreword

This is not an autobiography; it is a story of ideas and of a philosophy. I placed it in a historical context, which is the context of my life, out of which these ideas emerged. The intellectual endeavor will gain potency, and so will the notions produced, when contrasted with the hurdles I had to overcome to give them birth. My life may, on one hand, be seen as tragic and, on the other, as a triumph over adversity. I hope it will ultimately be a latter.

The ideas are important in themselves, and it was for themselves that I approached the task of conceiving them. Hopefully, that is how they will be seen by those who read this book. But the life I here describe will be briefly portrayed. The person who harmed or betrayed me will not be mentioned by name, as I do not wish to brood on grievances and give publicity to those people. The prisons I was incarcerated in will not be described, nor my life there. Mental homes will not be overly mentioned. The ideas that came out of these places will, however. They are the chief purpose of this book.

Of course, the type of life I have led cannot be recommended for most people. It seems an absolute miracle that I managed to live so long or produce anything intellectually worthwhile. But, as you will see, I have come not to believe in miracles or accidents. Because I infer that the world is necessary and ordered, I also believe in purpose; logical purpose. If the world was not as I portray it to be in this book, it would be as the existentialists claim it is.

Don't think that because the autobiography given here is so extended and devoid of anything philosophically original to start with, that is how the rest of the work will continue. This book is written for people who are interested in ideas, and then with how they emerge.

The best way to lead the philosophical life is not my way, but in the manner of the scholar who progresses through the educational system. Certainly, it will be the safest. Something of the original spark may however be lost pursuing this path, but not every intellectual life has to deliver a revolution in thought.

Hope may be offered in reading the following account for those who lead unconventional lives in the pursuit of an intellectual goal. That is all I can give

1. Trinidad and England 1955–1975

As my life ends, I want to show that an intellectual pursuit can redeem an otherwise disastrous series of occurrences that could have characterised it. You don't have to have a career, or a family; devote yourself to acquiring money, to have dignity or self-esteem. You can save yourself from being destroyed by sexuality, disability, mental illness and imprisonment. This is said not boastfully, but in realisation that your life can still have purpose, shape and meaning, so that your particular life is transcended, and a relative happiness attained, knowing that something has been done with and made of it. Finally, I hope that my parents could come to feel that their son was Worth conception.

I was born in 1955 in Trinidad, the West Indies, and delivered in a hospital somewhere in Port of Spain, the capital. My father was Jerome Rampersad a young journalist, and my mother was Mutrice Greaves. Both Catholics and I was the second child of what was to be a family of four children – two boys and two girls – Mary, the eldest, myself, Mitzi and Gerald.

Trinidad was still part of the British Empire at that time, and had a population of about one million people. It is a relatively big island, as far as the West Indies go, about the size of Lancashire. My mother told me afterwards that we had at least one servant in the home, so we were quite well off. Though she did say that 'everyone' had servants at that time. I remember her helping my sisters with their Latin homework when we were later in England, so she was well-educated, but I don't know what work she did in Trinidad.

My father was half-Indian and my mother, Negro. This means they brought together the two main groups that formed the island's population. 'Rampersad', I was in time to learn, meant 'food of the gods' in Hindi. I suppose it has the same roots as the ancient Greek 'ambrosia'.

My mother tells me I had asthma as a baby, which I outgrew, and that I was a very pretty child, which I also outgrew. I remember the taste of my baby food, as well as, later, the taste of the boiled egg I took to nursery school.

Childhood must have been a happy time, although my mother informed me that I had been a 'coward baby'. This probably refers to my attempts at walking. I sometimes stayed with my grandmother – universally called 'mother' – and we were later to live in England with her. She lived in a part of Port of Spain called Belmont – a dignified old woman and my mother's mother.

However, there were omens for the future which occurred in infant school. Before the age of six, I felt and must have displayed feelings of a physical type towards a little Indian boy in my kindergarten, and towards a white boy, who I laughed and cavorted with. I remember a black boy burning me with matches – he must have seen something I had no name for that others did not discern in me. That is how far back my peculiar sexuality can be traced, and I don't now feel any blame for it.

Something happened to cause my parents to separate, but not divorce, being Catholics, and in 1961 at the age of six, I took the boat to England, with my mother, my siblings, my grandmother, but not my father, who stayed in Trinidad. I was not to see him until the early '70s, when he visited England for a short time.

It was what thousands of West Indians were doing at this period, when most of the islands were gaining independence from Britain. What would have my life been like if we had not done this? A lot different, and in many ways much more limited. The disasters that subsequently occurred would be possibly total, and redeemed by nothing. Surely for me it was a good thing we came then.

Arriving in England, we at, first lived, with a landlord called Mr Singh, a Sikh man, and his family, whose children attended the same school as myself. It was St. Mary Magdalene's in Southwark, London. We lived in the same road later until I left secondary school. This was St. Thomas the Apostle, a Roman Catholic comprehensive which I went to in 1966. My sisters went to the same Grammar school, and my brother to a public school as a day boy on a scholarship. My mother taught secretarial skills at a college of further education.

I had a good schooling at St. Thomas's, coming first every year in the top class, until we were put in the 'grammar' stream in order to take the ordinary level exams at the age of fourteen and the advanced level exams at the age of sixteen – an age most of the boys left school at. I got eleven 'O' Levels and three 'A' Levels, in English, French and Geography, though I only graduated in these exams with low grades on the most part.

In secondary school, the seeds were sown for my future development. I was short and had worn glasses since the age of ten, so when I was unfortunately made a prefect at the age of fourteen, the boys simply would not obey me. I lost my temper many times and was laughed at mercilessly. Going home, and being alone in my room, I would weep copiously. Finally, I tore my prefect's badge off and refused to be one any longer.

But good things happened. I studied classical music up to the age of sixteen and loved it, and listened to the classical station of the BBC on the radio. In my later years at school, I obtained a Saturday job at a music library, which lent classical music discs. I went to the Opera in London. One of the best gifts my mother gave me for a birthday was an album of all Handel's Organ Concertos, which I had never come across before. It was a great pleasure of my adolescence to listen to these records repeatedly. At school I determined to become a composer, but later decided that you had to be talented and have an ear, which I lacked.

Earlier, and this lasted longer than my hope to be a composer, I wanted to write poetry. Poems of mine had won prizes in the local educational authority's competitions. As I grew older, the themes got darker and religious – the result of a Catholic school. Also, features of my later character began to emerge in the 'crushes' I had on various boys.

An unpleasant and life-long illness manifested itself as well, at the age of sixteen. This was epilepsy. I don't know what caused it, but it may have been the result of hitting my head on a goalpost whilst playing football. It was quite serious, though controlled with drugs, and expressed itself at different times in my life in different ways.

At the end of my schooldays, I did not know what I wanted to do, but I knew I wanted to do something 'great' with my life. It was an adolescent ambition, coming partly from reading a biography of Richard Wagner, and partly from reflections on my inevitable death, which I had contemplated for some time with foreboding.

Here is a poem, one of the last I wrote then, at least a part of it:

> What lies inside your armour, knight?
> The same as outside rolls.
> What do you seek?
> The Crystal Vault of Nothing is my goal.
> Your quest is foolish, well you know,
> For how can Nothing end?
> Tell me your deeper feeling now, my hollow friend.
> I feel an empty statue
> Sculpted in an absurd pose,
> And deep inside a squatting dwarf
> Who nothing sees or knows.
> Hollow Knight, where is your place?
> In the silent realms of Space.
> Hollow Knight, how are you feeling?
> My shape is burst, my skin is peeling.
> The atoms of my very being
> Spill asunder, fast are fleeing
> Far apart,
> And every region holds the pieces of my heart.

And so on. Depressing stuff, no? But I found from the poetry I was reading, that the modem kind did not rhyme often, and was a lot different from the type of verse I was writing. At last, I came to realise that I would not have a place in poetry as it was now written. I dropped reluctantly that ambition

But I managed to get admitted to university – Keele in the Midlands – one of only two boys in my year to go on to college. I went there, though, without a clear idea of what I wanted to do with my life and mostly for the reason of avoiding doing a job.

At the end of my school years and with the onset of adolescence, I started something which lasted many decades in my life, namely, voyeurism of women, who I gradually came to be interested in. I went to university in 1973, at the age of eighteen and this voyeurism lasted many years, eclipsing my homosexual feelings. I should have succumbed to these and entered a gay coterie at college; but as far as I knew, I was alone and certainly not proud. Homosexual sex had been legalised in the late sixties in Britain, but I was underage. I knew of no way to express these feelings legally.

I sometimes had followed girls around the streets when I was at school, but done nothing, and at Keele, would slip into the girls' halls of residence to watch them taking their showers, I being safely concealed elsewhere.

But at Keele, something momentous happened which would determine the course of my life. I entered university, aiming to study English and French; subjects I had done at 'A' Level at St. Thomas's. At Keele though there was what was called a 'foundation' year in which students would take courses for one year before they began their degrees, in the humanities and a scientific subject. This was to ensure they had an all-round educational grounding to be included in their four-year degree courses. I opted to do as one of my humanities, philosophy. I do not remember much about this year now, but at the end of it, I had changed my degree to Philosophy and French.

Taking my BA in Philosophy, I met two men who would be important to me later: Jonathan Dancy, a young, bespectacled tutor and lecturer at the time, and Professor Richard Swinburne. Both men were to write books which I would subsequently read, under different circumstances.

Dancy praised an essay I had written in my first year in philosophy, the second at university, and I studied Lemmon's 'Beginning Logic', an excellent and classic introduction to the subject, covering everything, from propositional calculus- the algebra of whole sentences – to class theory – the logic of 'sets' or characterised collections. It ended with something I wasn't to comprehend for over a decade, namely Russell's Paradox, which Bertrand Russell himself said lay at the bottom of reasoning. Therefore, I decided what I would do with my life henceforth. I remember saying to myself at the age of nineteen: 'I will become competent in this'. By 'this' I meant philosophy.

I had for one year a normal course in the various areas of philosophy: the Greeks, the Modems – starting with Descartes, and proceeding along to Hume, with paradoxes in causation and induction, the latter being the logic of practical reasoning. We even studied Kant and were introduced to his ethical theory. I remember Dancy pointing to a copy of Kant's 'Groundwork to the Metaphysics of Morals', a slim little volume, and saying, 'That is one of the great books.'

Something however would emerge during my time at Keele which was to plague my life; it had happened in school during my unhappy time as a prefect and would dog me later. This was a proneness to lose my temper when I felt I was being mocked or was really being mocked; I came not to be able to tell the difference.

Continuing on more pleasant themes, we studied Wittgenstein, where he is contrasted with Plato, whose Theory of Forms dominated Western thought in various guises for many ages. The latter holds that things are the sorts of things they are by 'participating' in the perfect archetype that exists in a transcendent, more real realm. These are 'Forms'. Wittgenstein, in his posthumously published book, 'Philosophical Investigations', holds that things do not possess features that are common to all of their kind, such that one overriding 'Universal', which may or may not be real, is to be posited to explain them. They only have 'family resemblances' which are more or less strong, and by which we collect them into kinds

I studied well and mostly enjoyably in Philosophy and French for the first year at Keele, and at the end of the third term took something I would have to take every year until the finals, namely my sessional tests in both subjects. On the morning of the philosophy exam, I awoke in my room in the halls of residence, early. I decided to go back to sleep. When I awoke again, I found I had overslept and missed much of the exam, which I only managed to complete one half of. When my results came, I had failed the philosophy exam. I therefore had to re-sit it, but that would be later on, and I had to return to my home in London to pass the time. Unfortunately, my mother had gone on holiday to France and was unavailable to pay for my transport back to the Midlands. Contemplating the loss of my degree course and an inability to continue studying philosophy, I felt suicidal. I went to a local social security office to hopelessly plead for money to avert these disasters. The refusal made me cause a disturbance, which led to a tussle and, feeling enraged and in despair, went back to my home nearby and took a cricket bat and a carving knife, intending to cause as much damage at the social security office as possible. The police were called, and one of them, a big officer, wrestled me to the ground and tried to arrest me.

I stabbed him three times in the thigh, and he limped off. His name was Ian Wheeler, and I felt no animosity to either him personally or to the police in general, and I feel sorry for the harm I did him. I did harm to myself, for I initiated by that action a lifetime of criminal implications, with the consequent imprisonment, further dealings with the police on the false premise that I had something against them, and homelessness and joblessness.

I was sentenced on a charge of grievous bodily harm to serve three years in prison, of which I would have to serve two years. This is a natural break for my history to take; at the age of twenty-one in 1976, I had laid the grounds for my education and direction in life; a life my mother told me in tears at the prison, that I had ruined. I asked her not to see me again whilst I was serving my sentence, and I faced the future alone. I continued suffering from and being treated for epilepsy, and it was in prison that my mental life would take a turn that might have been foreseen in my university days, but at the time seemed to involve no definite plan to it.

2. The Project: Prison 1975–1980

I started a process of self-discovery when I was locked in solitary confinement for some misdemeanour. Being allowed books again, I started to think and read philosophy. A book I obtained was AJ Ayer's *Language, Truth and Logic,* which introduced the theories of the Vienna Circle to England in the 1930s. I enjoyed its style of philosophy, which was to argue for every proposition, give a conceptual reason why a statement should be believed. It became my own method in time.

But I remembered things I had encountered in Keele. One was the Ontological Argument for the existence of God, which was invented by St. Anselm, Archbishop of Canterbury in the 12th Century, and taken up by several rationalist philosophers in modern times, starting with Descartes. He said that one should think of God as a being who necessarily existed because he was something that contained all 'perfections'. Existence was one of these because not to exist would be to be less perfect than to exist. Therefore, God, by definition, had to exist and he could not be doubted.

Variations on this argument, and on Anselm's version, which in some ways is more subtle and compelling, have been posited even in recent times by philosophers. But a possible refutation was offered by Kant in his book, *The Critique of Pure Reason*. He maintained that 'existence' was not a real predicate. A predicate is anything said of the thing a sentence referred to and which describes it. In classical logic, one pointed to the world, indicating a particular item – the subject – and said something of it – the predicate. If existence cannot be a real predicate, and Kant offers examples of how it cannot be one, it cannot be a 'perfection' of God and the ontological argument is falsified.

However, there may be alternatives to this which rescue the argument, and these have been seized on by other modem philosophers who want to accept it.

The ontological argument – 'ontos', the Greek for 'being'- is something that I am sure troubles many students commencing their courses, and it troubled me alone in my cell.

Again, there was David Hume's 18th Century scepticism on causality and induction. He held that no one event had to cause another because each fact was a distinct and independent existence. The necessary connection, which was the principal element in his analysis of the relation between cause and effect, simply was not observed. Also, it was possible to doubt whether any object had to cause any other event and therefore it was possible because conceivable. If it was necessary that one fact had to be the cause of another, the negative would be inconceivable; but it was not, so 'causes' could not be posited.

But it was the problem of induction for which his scepticism is most famous. Induction is factual reasoning of the kind which argues from a particular instance of something to a general rule. This could be from experience of the past to projections onto the future; e.g. 'The Sun will rise tomorrow'. Or it could be experience from a limited region of space, to a projection onward to all regions of space. This type of reasoning is the basis of much science and common behaviour, and it is counterintuitive to doubt it. Logic, however, shows it can be doubted. The inductive transitions from the particular to the universal cannot be · validated by deductive reasoning. In deductive reasoning, if an assumption is true, the conclusion is always true. But there is no reason of this kind to say that an inductive argument is valid. In inductive reasoning, a true assumption may lead to a false conclusion. Our experience cannot be called upon to validate inductive reasoning, for it will itself use inductive assumptions. And since we can imagine the opposite of an inductive argument, or at least the negative of the conclusion, then it is logically possible that what we project does not happen.

I thrashed around in my mind trying to work these conclusions out. I could not accept them, yet I could not refute them. It is the position philosophy has found itself in since. 'The solution to the. Problem of ·· induction is that it has no solution'. We have to use induction, but we cannot justify it.

I read what I could in my cell, and asked for notebooks, which I filled with my cogitations on these puzzles. If logic arrived at a paradox, then something must be wrong with the assumptions logic uses.

I conceived of something I called the 'exclusion arguments', that these assumptions must be radically revised: time, space, existence and identity. These I felt held the key to the problem. Then I recollected the vision of Bishop

Berkeley, a philosopher who preceded Hume in the 18th Century. He denied 'material substance' in the world and he felt that things were just collections of qualities. He thought that those who proposed 'substance' meant by it 'being in general', along with the notion of its supporting attributes. But as he also rejected abstract ideas and thought that being in general was the 'most abstract and incomprehensible' of all abstract ideas, he said that those who proposed substance could attach no meaning to their words. It was as if things did not need 'being' to 'support' them and make them real.

Then I had very little to do to have the inspiration I had later on in my cell. I mouthed to myself: 'Things do not exist.' That I knew was the revelation the denial of which had been the essential fallacy in conceptual thought throughout time.

My mind was working overtime, and inspiration after inspiration flowed into it. What were things if they did not exist? Things were their natures. Things were how they are, not that they are. What was the meaning of 'existence'? At first, and for a long time afterwards, I thought that it meant 'universe membership'.

I determined to devote myself and my life to solving the problems of causation and induction, for these ideas were the key to the solution. Since things did not exist, they could not be distinct existences. If things were 'how' they are, then changes have to be 'how' they are rather than 'that' they are. They had to come about physically. If existence was removed from the world, so was the lack of necessity or 'contingency' it brought into the world. For what I called a 'physical description' of nature could not propound the lack of compulsion that attaches to existence because, despite the ontological argument, it has been almost universally held by thinkers that existence is not necessary. 'Whatever is may not be'. That is why the ontological argument is so paradoxical. And this argument is refuted if existence is not anything God could have.

I underestimated the complexity of the task, but I felt that this belief in existence was the reason for scepticism about causality and practical reasoning. I knew that I had in effect commenced with the solution to the difficulty and had to fill in the implications. I would not aim to get a job or have a career, because they would distract me in my goal. Besides, my epilepsy would prevent that, and it was with single minded determination, but with many diversions on the way, that I entered upon this lifetime's project. The purpose was purely intellectual; the solving of something akin to a mathematical problem.

When I came to leave prison, I had filled many notebooks with writing on these topics. Looking back, I marvel at how precarious this intellectual aim and purpose was. So many things could and did intervene subsequently to side-track me and cause my failure. Yet it was my source of strength: it has given my life motivation and a reason. In no way is it to be despised as an alternative to earning money and getting a home, for these things die with one but, if achieved, it attains nobility and can last.

I went back home and it was arranged that I fly to Trinidad to live with my father, who my mother had got to write to me in prison. My father, called 'Boyee' by his brothers and relations, was a stern, unhappy man, who had lost his job on the Trinidad Guardian for union activity, and had a job, a 'sinecure' he called it, on the local radio station as news editor. We did not hit it off, for I was also unhappy and silent.

When he learnt I wanted to do philosophy, he told me that all I could do with it was teach. Trinidad was not quite the intellectual backwater I had come to expect from my reading of V.S. Naipaul's travel writings, for I later found books by the logician W.V.O.Quine and others.

I came not to like my father, who lived alone in an apartment and never smiled. When I, demonstrating a tendency I had not outgrown, got into a quarrel at a cinema, and went back to the apartment to seize a cosh my father kept for intruders, I was arrested and injected with a sedative by a doctor and spent several days in a state of utter prostration in a mental hospital. Later, I went to a day hospital, and when at home got so much on my father's nerves that he threatened to call the mental home and have me sectioned. When I was in the day hospital the next day, I brooded on this· threat and wished for my father's death. And got home in the evening and saw him lying on his bed. I went to my room. Friends and relations came as they often did, and discovered that my father was in fact dead. Later, we learned, it was of a stroke.

My relations paid for my return to England, where my mother got me a job working in a light-engineering factory as a general labourer, and she got me a place to live in ·a Y.M.C.A hostel.

A quarrel with fellow workers about my homosexuality led to a second trial for threatening behaviour and possession of an offensive weapon. The police tried to make it more serious but a clever lawyer showed the jury that the more serious charges were concocted because I was known to them as someone who had injured a colleague.

Meanwhile, I had spent 3 months in prison on remand. I was sentenced to probation. Going home again, my mother professed herself surprised at the behaviour of the police, and my brother, who never liked my manifestations of homosexuality and my prison sentence, said I was 'corrupt', as he put it.

Several weeks later my mother told me that in three-months' time she wanted me to set myself up with a job. It was a reasonable request, but I took it as a signal that she did not like me. I gathered my belongings - books, notes and other things - in two suitcases and stormed out of the house; my younger sister, Mitzi, pressed a twenty-pound note into my hands, and I never saw them again, since the age of 23, an age, I am sure, by which most children have left home.

I tramped the streets, homeless and destitute, carrying in two arms my heavy suitcases with my precious notes. Until they got too heavy for me, and I dumped one suitcase with my books from university but kept my writing books. I continued constantly to think about intellectual problems and would add jottings to my manuscript books of the thoughts that occasionally came to me.

I got to Parliament Square one day and was picked up by policemen. I was foolish enough to tell them that I had stabbed a policeman, and there and then they concocted a charge of resisting arrest and assault. I was bailed, but did not go to court at the appointed time, thinking the charge was too stupid even to contemplate. In a hostel run by a charity who took me in and gave me a bed, several months later, I managed to get into a dispute with another client who phoned the police. Arrested, I was taken to a police station where my outstanding charge was identified, the one for which I was bailed to appear at court. I was again imprisoned on remand for about five months and found guilty at trial and given probation. So in five years since 1975 I had been imprisoned three times, though two were for periods of remand.

Even in prison I continued with my thoughts and had kept a manuscript book in the hands of a friendly probation officer – Arthur Ashby. I remember when I told him that I was solving the problem of induction and causality, he had objected, 'What about Entropy?' He also asked if my arguments in my notebook were in question-and-answer form; whether I made objections to them and replied to them. This, despite my reading of A J Ayer, was a tendency lacking from my work. There was too much pure assertion without a reason given for them.

A provisional title for my thesis was 'At Dreaming's End', a quotation from the translation into English of 'Also Sprach Zarathustra' by Nietzsche. The Midnight Song contains the lines:

> I've slept my sleep
> And now awake at dreaming's end…

I kept this title for years.

But towards the end of those five years, I came to reflect on the analysis of causation Hume had made. He included 'necessary connection' in the common idea between one event and another. Not only was it not observable, but logically it could not be shown to obtain since the denial of a causal relation was perfectly conceivable. I thought, and the idea stole upon me slowly, 'Of course things must be related or connected'. It was self-evident and intuitive, though these were not good enough philosophical reasons for saying why.

In philosophy it is often very difficult to give logical reasons for the intuitive. I had however to do so.

The next few years, the years of the eighties decade, were to be characterised for me by association with the mental health system. Sometimes I went to mental homes as schizophrenia and anxiety evidenced themselves; this was in addition to chronic epilepsy, for which I took pills. In the next years I continued, with breaks, to do my saving philosophy, and it was towards the end to re-emerge in a much different and strengthened form.

Meanwhile, I was out of society since 1975, and had missed the Punk revolution in popular culture. I was no longer a virgin, but started going to prostitutes. They could handle my sexual weakness without mocking me, for I was, if not actually, almost completely impotent. I also consorted with men I met in public lavatories. If I had not met up with prostitutes, I would still be a virgin and I have always paid for sex with women.

This is a natural break in my narrative and the eighties form a distinct period in my philosophy's development and in my progress.

3. Years of Madness
1980–1989

Released from prison a third time, I was a homeless vagrant. I squatted in an abandoned factory in the Croydon area of London. I left my manuscripts in the keeping of Mr Ashby, my probation officer, who from time to time would write out small cheques from his expenses and give me money for a meal. Otherwise, I stole milk and bread left in front gardens. One night, in the depths of my desolation, I saw the moon shining, and it was very big. I lost awareness and the next thing I knew, when I came to myself, I found that I was in a place I later knew was Warlingham Park Hospital for the mentally disturbed. This was a place I visited occasionally for the next few years. Years in which I gained friends I met in the mental health system, though they were not significant in the production of my philosophy. Also I had a few jobs for brief periods, and of menial kinds.

After several months, I was given a place in a half-way home in Kent for mentally ill, but recovering, young people. I had a room to myself then and could observe the world I had been out of for so long, on television. The Falklands War was taking place, but other things occupied my mind. Why were things necessarily related? The reason was, I was sure, because the nature of a 'world' demanded it. Merely by being parts of a world, and in order to form a world, things had to have access, one to another. It was conceptually necessary. A world would be impossible if things had no relations; so given a world, relations were necessary.

I called this argument by various names, starting in prison where it had originated: the 'universe' argument was one. This later became the 'world' argument. And it was one of the effects of existence that it separated things. If things did not exist necessarily, nothing else could make them exist. Existence was never in the natures of things – a reason why it was not necessary. So a thing could not be necessitated in its existence by another thing, or caused. This directly clashed with the 'world' argument, so either existence or 'world' would have to go. 'World' engendered cause because it engendered necessary connection. This was the foundation for my insight in prison that the belief in existence led to causal scepticism.

It seemed to me that the world, or a world, was self-evident. It also seemed a logical demand that a plurality meant that the elements in it had access to one another·. Existence was to be rejected. These ideas were generated over time and their development interrupted by a period of further incarceration in the mental hospital for a psychotic collapse.

The 'world' argument was to occupy my mind for the next few years. It was a time in which I got residence in several hostels for the mentally ill at different times and for different lengths of time. The longest was three years spent at one in the throes of and in thrall to anxiety. The latter involved panic attacks during which a nameless, unfocused fear would creep over me, and at its height, I would be rendered speechless, or at best, monosyllabic.

I, during the period 1984 to 1987, reached my nadir mentally. I was resident at a hostel in Croydon and recognised, as I had done soon after going into the first hostel in Kent, that I really wanted a university education. I felt half-educated otherwise. In Kent I had tried to return to Keele University, but they would not accept me. But later on in Croydon, I realised that I could not study at university level as long as I suffered from this terrible anxiety.

A psychologist at the day hospital I attended diagnosed anxiety, but said it would pass. Meantime, my despair caused me to attempt suicide, when I took a week's supply of epilepsy tablets at once. I passed out and was revived in hospital, but did damage as a result to my brain. I was unable henceforth to have more than what is called 'twilight' sleep. This meant that I could no longer get fully unconscious at night, but at best would dream profoundly.

I did however recover mentally, and the anxiety disappeared. Taking to heart the sense that my arguments in my philosophy, needed counter- arguments, which could be met, I wondered if it was conceivable that the ' world' ·argument was wrong, for some unidentified reason. What if the world consisted of objects that simply existed and needed no necessary relativity?

My philosophy had been somewhat in abeyance during this latter period of my problems with anxiety, but it started up again with renewed vigour. Surely things in being real were also relatively real to other real things. But consider existence, which it was said caused this reality; not only did it lead to relevance to other things in a physical sense, but it also led to contingency, which meant independence. That was a contradiction. From my year of philosophy at Keele, I had learnt of the 'reductio ad absurdum' proof, whereby if an assumption led to a contradiction, one could negate the assumption as false. Since existence led to a contradiction, it must be rejected, and something else should be responsible for things' reality. Therefore existence was not reality. Things were real, but they did not exist.

I spent a relatively short time working out the implications of this argument, and produced reasons to support it further. It proved causality because it proved it merely from the need for mutual relevance among real things. And it disproved existence by showing it was responsible for paradox. I came to call this chapter of my growing thesis, 'Paradoxes of Existence'.

But something was to occur towards the end of 1987, when I was recovering my mental equilibrium. I have always found I did my best work when I was most normal, and normality was returning.

In my reading that I was doing at that time, I came upon Russell's Paradox, which so baffled me since Keele. A class is a set of things characterized by common factors. To say a thing had a certain predicate was to say it was a member of a certain class. There are rules for membership of a class, one of which is to possess the relevant property. There are different kinds of set just as there are different kinds of thing. Some contain solid, real things; some are abstract collections. A set or class is thought to be an abstract object. The logicist movement among logicians and mathematicians, at the start of the 20th Century, held that all mathematics was reducible to logic, and one of the axioms it held was that for every predicate there was a class that exemplified it. Sets, or classes; are used in an advanced kind of mathematics, and numbers can be defined in terms of sets. What, Russell asked in his paradox, about the class of classes that are not members of themselves? Some classes are members of themselves, like the class of abstract objects; some are not – the class of rocks is not a. rock. The class of classes that are not members of themselves, is a member of itself if it is not, and is not a member of itself if it is. Paradox.

For many years I did not understand the paradox, which, if valid, meant that every predicate does not have its own set. There could be no such set. To be a member of itself means to have the predicate it exemplifies. Not to be a member of itself means not to have the predicate that it is the extension of. What it was 'to be a member' was what baffled me. And the self-reference threw me.

Once I saw the reasoning behind the paradox, which meant that the logicist programme was overthrown, it did not seem so difficult to me. But it had been the starting-point of higher logic. If logic contained a paradox, something must be wrong with the assumptions of logic. Russell said this paradox afflicted the very basis of reasoning. Attempts to solve the paradox had been made ever since.

I was writing the Overview to my theories so far, in order to collect them together into a manageable form. I had used the definition I offered of existence, Universe Membership, and said that things could not belong, or be members, because of belonging; and this was an argument against contingency. Things could not exist just because they existed; things could not belong merely because of belonging.

Then I saw the answer to the paradox. In it, membership was made the reason for membership merely by being the criterion for itself. It was its own reason. Membership and its negation, non-membership, cannot be predicates. Why? Because membership had no nature, it has nothing to characterise it. Not recognising this became the essence of what I was later to call, the Membership Fallacy. .

It was a great day for me when I discerned this. I knew I was on to something exceptional. For membership was a logical operator; it was part of the most exact part of philosophy – logic. I had discovered the logical basis of the existential fallacy. I could use logic to show that existence was invalid. For if membership was invalid, if it was also existence, then existence was invalid. Membership was not only a fallacy because it had no nature, but because it led to paradox. If membership was wrong, then the whole of set theory, or classes, was also wrong. My philosophy would be placed on a logical, nay, a mathematical footing.

At the end of '87, when my time at the hostel I had stayed at was drawing to a close because I was getting better, I was to be transferred to a half-way flat of my own before being given a council flat. There, just by chance, and in one of the most fortunate strokes of luck that could be imagined, I happened upon a final issue of an intellectual periodical. One of its articles was a fictional, comic account of a meeting at Cambridge between Bertrand Russell and Ludwig Wittgenstein. I remember something Wittgenstein is made to say to Russell, reclining in a deckchair: 'They came to the tomb and found it empty. That is the true mystery! Not how things are but that they are·. Tell me Russell, why is there something rather than *just* nothing, why is there anything at all?' Russell replies: 'How am I meant to know? I'm a mathematician, not God almighty! -' I had heard-it said that God was a mathematician, and that the Universe was a mathematical object. Still, questions of this kind had been occupying me for years.

Also, I read somewhere in the magazine an advertisement made by the Open University. It was for a course, lasting eight months, in modern philosophy, called 'Reason and Experience': the continental rationalists and the British empiricists.

I applied for the course and was accepted, though I was on benefit, saw a psychiatrist regularly and was suffering from epilepsy. Every month the class would meet at the London School of Economics for lectures and otherwise study at home. I enjoyed the course and passed well. I met people there who were going to use that course at the Open University to get into other universities to do a full degree. My psychiatrist told me: 'Use a minnow to catch a whale'.

I opted for Birkbeck College, University of London, and a friend of mine, a former policeman, a young man called Paul Wolward, who I met at the Open University, chose the School of Oriental and African Studies to do a philosophy degree at. Birkbeck was for mature students who paid for the degree course lasting four years, and had lectures in the evening. I was to ·get a charitable grant from an organisation because of my extreme poverty. All this I learned before I started the course in 1989.

But before Birkbeck commenced, and before I could move into my council flat at the same time, I got into trouble with the law again for carrying an offensive weapon, which I had threatened a pornographic shop owner with, who had mocked and 'rooked' me. I still betrayed a propensity I had not lost to brood upon mockery and insults. I was fined £20 and put on probation.

I got over this however and re-entered university at the age of thirty-four in 1989 to do a degree course in philosophy. There was also a move to a council flat, a bedsit. This was a place I was to stay at for the next five years.

Birkbeck was certainly a prestigious place; set in West London, near Tottenham Court Road, it contained some well-known philosophers, not the least of whom was Roger Scruton, professor of Aesthetics. I had read one of his books, an introduction to modern philosophy, whilst at the hostel. He was a well-known commentator on aesthetics, or the philosophy of art and beauty, and he appeared not infrequently on the radio and television. He was a political commentator and a right-wing intellectual who worked for the Conservative Party, then in power for ten years; he aided the highest echelons of power and spoke one dozen languages. His doctoral thesis had been 'Art and Imagination', and I admired him much. This was not reciprocated, for my displays of homosexual tendencies, manifested in voyeurism at the college, alienated and repelled him. He, at that time, was a tall man with a shock of red hair and glasses. His feelings towards me did not obscure his appreciation of any intellectual merit he might perceive me to possess.

There were others there: Professor David Wiggins, a noted ethicist and all-round thinker, whose book 'Sameness and Substance', argued for the re-introduction into Western thought of the notion of substance. And Samuel Guttenplan, who had written a best-selling introduction to logic that our first-year course in it was to be based on. He was an American, much admired by his students.

I had gone to university this time for the sake of my thesis, which by then had been collated in a thick manuscript book. The degree I was aiming for would be got by my research during the seventies and eighties for my theories, and by the original thinking I had done, which was extensive. I read during that time much theoretical physics and cosmology, because it was relevant to any metaphysics about the world and causation and induction. I also knew about – and had theories related to my thought – linguistic philosophy, which dominated the English-speaking world in much of the twentieth century. This philosophy rejected metaphysics as meaningless because unverifiable, but I thought the linguistic turn in thought self-referential and decadent. What I was doing was firmly in the tradition of Western metaphysics: it was about the world; but it had to make use of and not ignore, the developments made in philosophy in the twentieth century. ·

By the time the four years of my course were up, my theory would be complete and it amazes me now how much thinking I managed to get into it in those four years. Every summer I would revise my writing in a new, big manuscript book, and all the time I reflected. Roger Scruton came to 'like' me, but he was a stern man who once said he tolerated homosexuality, but did not like it.

At that time I met and befriended Fiona Ellis, in the year above me, ten years younger and brilliant. She stayed my friend all through the nineties and even into the dark days beyond when I fell back into the pit. All these people, and others, were to help me in my thinking for my thesis. I shall indicate the ideas in and implications of my thesis, at least in part. This story is not meant as an autobiography but as a history of ideas. It is the tale of a philosophy and an explanation of it. The culmination of my thinking arrived in the nineties when, for the most part, all went well for me. So to this decade I proceed, but not forgetting the work done philosophically in the two preceding ones.

4. Redemption
1989–1999

Some of the ideas I mention here originated in the two years between 1987 and 1989, but I include them in the decade I describe. For many years I had seen existence as 'universe membership'; but a more exact examination of membership led me to change my mind. The universe was a world of physical things and these were, as I had said, how they were not that they were. Membership was a relation, and membership had to be of a class of some kind. It could not be of the class of physical things, which membership was not, but had to be of a class that ensured that membership had no nature. To ensure membership was pure it had to be membership of the class of class members. That was what existence was, for it likewise, had no nature. Membership would cause chaos if allowed to be a predicate or a reason for membership of a class: anything with it could get into any class whatever. So membership had to be quarantined and apply to a characterless class. But really, it was an impossible concept, with an impossible class. Just as membership was a pseudo relation, membership of the class of class-members was membership of a pseudo-class. The elements in such a class had no nature, and so could not be collected.

I was able to show that membership was existence, logically. In class theory we expressed non-existence by saying that the class of the non-existent objects was. 'empty', that is, memberless. So to express an object's existence we should say that its class was not-memberless. Thus membership was existence. Also, asserting belonging to a determinate class was predication. The pre-condition for determinate belonging and the pre-condition for predication were the same. The pre-condition for determinate belonging was pure belonging, and the pre-condition for predication was existence. These identified. And since membership, existence, had no nature, it could not belong to anything; so membership, existence, implied non-membership, non-existence. This was the source of the long-held belief that existence was nothing.

Another long-lasting dispute, from the beginning of Western philosophy, was 'the· monism-pluralism debate. Monism held that there was one thing, and pluralism that there were many. This was resolvable if existence was membership. Having no nature, members could not form a class, because there was nothing in virtue of which they could be related or connected; so members were isolated and distinct, utterly. But a nature allowed things to be collected and classed. A class of both members and things with a nature would be isolated in terms of members and, if these members were also nature-possessing, collected. This was a contradiction of external relations, relations that were not inherent to the things related. Pluralism maintained such relations, so the dispute between it and monism was resolved in favour of monism. Atomism; the belief in individuals that were simple and isolated from each other that went with pluralism, was refuted.

I later came to see this argument meant that in a world without membership in the form of existence, things had to transcend pure particularity and be non-particular as well: they had to have universality. This was a way of establishing induction, for the problem of induction required us to see things as atomic individuals with no possibility of allowing general, universal statements being made of them.

The membership fallacy caused the fallacy of existence, and it caused others. I showed this by examining, over a period, logical, linguistic, even mathematical paradoxes. The Liar paradox was suspicious; it looked just like Russell's, and it did not take long for me to see that Truth too was membership, therefore had no nature and was an impossible notion. It goes like this: if we say, 'This statement is false', then we can derive that if 'this statement' is true, it is false, and if it is false, it is true. All theories of truth are susceptible to the Liar paradox. Truth is reduced to absurdity by the paradox; and so is, of course, Falsehood.

So what was Truth? I determined that to say a sentence was 'true' was to say that it 'belonged' linguistically. The physical situation described by a sentence was supposed to belong in reality to the world and thus it 'belonged' and existed. The sentence reflected this by reproducing the physical state of affairs and reproducing its belonging mediately, by means of language, both to the world and purely. I could show that truth, membership and existence were identical: if an object, any object, 'fell under' a concept, then one, a concept was 'instantiated', two, a concept 'was true of an object' – understanding 'F is true of x' to be equivalent to 'x is F is true' - and three, an object was a member of the extension of a concept. The quoted formulas said the same thing. For a concept to be 'instantiated' was to assert existence. Other historical metaphysical arguments were found.

These paradoxes were examined in the years of my recovering from anxiety and going to university again. The membership fallacy ran through the whole of philosophy. Cantor's paradox, named after an important 19th Century German mathematician, was solvable. It was solvable if classes were rethought. They could not contain real things and yet be abstract objects, but had to run over ideas, sub-ideas, if they were to retain their abstractness. And these sub-ideas mirrored sub-classes; they replaced them. Members were to be excluded.

I examined paradox after paradox, some linguistic, some mathematical, all in order to express and fortify the point about the membership fallacy, which in some way was responsible for them all. Because classes with membership contained real things and were real objects, they could contain themselves. What was called 'self-predication' was always going to be possible with membership; and it was directly responsible for Russell's paradox and the others. But in solving Cantor's paradox, I had rethought classes as containing sub-ideas derived from 'originals' or real things outside the class. At the top of the abstractive progression that was the class was the Notion or Intension. Classes can be seen theoretically as a collection of objects, or as the meaning, the 'intension', of the concept or predicate that those things are collected under. This is in the conventional theory of classes. I had a 'notional' or 'intensional' theory. Sub-ideas, or sub-classes, were included in classes and within the class itself, a notion could only identify with itself. It could not be included in itself or have itself as a predicate. This was because the Notion or class was at the top of the tree, in terms of abstraction, so could not itself be one of those things it was abstracted from. It was self-identified.

My thinking was getting more metaphysical now, but I was still able to include the membership fallacy in it. Things were not existent, but the reason why they were real was because they were how they were, because they had a nature. Not existing meant, not that they were nothing, but that they neither 'existed' nor 'not-existed'. They were beyond both, like the God of the Sufi mystics. When existence went, so did non-existence. Neither was possible.

My thought had gone far from being a simple examination of cause and induction, but I was able to bring it back for a while. The world was not a collection of particular individuals. Collections meant members, and the world did not have membership in the form of existence. This meant that the world, without membership, must be a systematic unity. I was able to solve inductive and causal paradoxes at a stroke. Things were connected of necessity and they transcended particularity, so any description of them could not break them up into isolated bits, either of space, time, or instance. A rule for a time was a rule for all time.

The world was what I called the 'qualitative' world or 'descriptive' world, being a thing containing items that were how they were. A change in events had to be how it was. That is, it had to be physical. It did not just come into being but was brought about: it physically arose; there was a reason for it. That was 'cause'. But was it necessary? Here, going to Birkbeck and encountering sharp minds proved useful and essential in the development of my ideas. I had long said, yes:

if that was how something was, that was how it had to be. If the colour Green was green, it had to be green. Fiona Ellis pointed out to me when I said this to her, 'But it's trivial, It was a tautology, something not really applicable to the world.'

I went away to cogitate about this, for I knew I was right in the end. I saw that when the criterion of necessity to exist was applied to my arguments, they failed. But when the world no longer existed, but was how it was, the criterion for necessity could not any longer be the necessity to exist, but was the necessity to be how one was. And things in the world satisfied this demand. Red could have existed instead of Green, but in its nature Red could not have been Green, or any other thing. A triangle was a geometrical form; Red was a wavelength of light. Things had to be how they were in the descriptive world; they were necessary. The criterion had changed. Tautology was avoided.

This meant that physical events, causes, relations, and so forth, were necessary, being what I named 'descriptive'.

The changes, causes that happened had non-particular aspects. When it was observed that A was physically followed by B, this could be expanded into a rule that A was always followed by B, non-particularly. This showed induction to be a logical, not a psychological practice. But of course, epistemological impediments arose in these cases: we could always get the relationship between A and B wrong; but the point was that Induction was established as a logically valid practice even if inductions could not be so justified.

The 'descriptive' world needed attention given to itself. One could hardly reject a concept as wide-ranging as existence and not say what the concept that replaced it made the resulting world like. Because the world did not exist, it was not brought into existence. It was not created. Also, because it transcended being and nothingness, it did not have the possibility of being nothing. It must be something; but that meant be descriptive and nature-possessing; and it was necessarily real since being descriptive was the only possibility.

There were difficulties that arose in my mind concerning the things in this world. These difficulties concerned change, which I had to explain. Things could not come into being or go out of being. Associated with Change were problems about Identity. I defined two senses of the word 'identity'. One was as 'uniqueness' in the sense found in such sentences as: 'The nations of Europe should retain their national identity'. The other was more problematic, in the sense of relational identity or sameness, as in: 'A is identical to B'. The latter seemed to be a predication of something of itself. It seemed to be a self-predication.

I was able to see the first sense and the second in existential terms, when the membership fallacy operated. Uniqueness was a product of the isolation and distinctness of members from each other. Relational identity was a self-predication of a class to itself. When a thing was unique, it was like a universe or set, and the only thing it could belong to was itself. But we had seen that self-predication was illegitimate, and replaced by self-identity in logic: it was another way of expressing self - identity. So both senses of identity were definable in terms of existence and membership. And I had to re-express identity in a descriptive manner.

Another way in which the membership fallacy appeared was in the ancient idea of Substance. All the features of substance were explainable by membership. It was a form of membership. Indeed, all the concepts that lacked a nature had to be the same thing, for only in virtue of a nature could they be different.

I went back to Necessity, and saw that, because the descriptive world was real, its necessity could not be in an abstract form, but identified with how things were, with situations themselves. Reality was Necessity. Old questions like, 'Why is there something rather than just nothing, why is there anything at all?' which Wittgenstein had asked Russell in the comic and fictional debate, were answerable. Because things were beyond being and non-being, Necessity was now necessity to be how one was. And the question was not: 'Need the world be?', but: 'Need the world be how it is?' The answer was 'Yes'. The world was necessary, but not necessarily existent; it was necessarily how it was. The way things were was necessary. Things, the world, were not created.

I saw that the old philosophical dictum that experience gave one no idea of necessity, was wrong. For experience of reality was experience of necessity. We knew if and how something was necessary by knowing that it was real.

These were deep areas, and my thought grew more and more metaphysical as I progressed. I had thought that analytic statements were necessary, like thousands of other thinkers before me. 'Analytic' statements were statements where the concept of the subject contained the predicate of the sentence. But I had rejected 'truth' and replaced it with 'analyticity'. I contrasted it to self-contradiction – a natural opposition – and that replaced 'falsity'. Meanings were objective, and things gave the subjects of sentences their meanings independently of ourselves. There was however the problem of necessity. In the existential world, any description of it would be contingent. So how could an analytic statement describe it if it was necessary? This occupied me for a long time; then I saw that the nature of the world gave sentences their necessity or contingency: their 'modality'. In respect to analyticity or contradiction, these were neutral in terms of modality. Depending on the 'world one accepted, an analytic sentence could be necessary – the Descriptive one – or could be contingent – the existential one. It was a great revolution in my thought to grasp that analytic sentences could be contingent, that analyticity and self-contradiction could be modally neutral.

The membership fallacy manifested itself also in the concept of reference. Asserting reference, for instance, for subjects of sentences, was to assert existence; and asserting failure of reference was asserting non-existence. But existence and non-existence were membership and non-membership; consequently asserting reference or its lack was asserting membership or its negation. The argument was more complex than this, but it was essentially simple. Reference was membership. But if that was so, self-reference was self-membership, which was self-predication. If the case, then in the intensional theory of classes, it was illogical, and though possible in membership, was ultimately wrong because membership was fallacious.

Reference was linguistic, and of course membership appeared in other areas of philosophy like metaphysics and logic. But reference was a way of acquiring meaning; and self-predication was similar. But if talking about something outside the sentence was the ultimate way of meaning-acquisition, or talking about the world, then talking about oneself, as in self-reference, implied meaninglessness. This must be the final solution to all self-referential paradoxes: they were meaningless.

In Godel's Theorem, which destroyed the logicist programme, it was stated that: in any system of logic that can express the mathematical truths, if it was complete, it would not be consistent, and if consistent would not be complete. That is to say, for such a system, if it could express all the propositions of maths, it would have paradoxes in it; and if it didn't have paradoxes, it would not express all the propositions of mathematics. However, in the proof of this theorem, Godel used quite essentially a self-referential formula. This meant that it was meaningless. It was outside the scope of the logical system; it was not a possible formula within that system, so could not say anything about or affect that system. Possibly, one impediment to the enterprise of reducing mathematics to logic was removed.

I reflected some more on the nature of philosophical inquiry. What made abstract concepts and abstract arguments apply to the world? Why should we believe them? I saw that my arguments, say for causality and induction, applied to my concept of the world, and only if this concept mirrored the real world was it likely to be valid. The order in the world generated conceptual thinking, I believed, and there were reasons for believing in order; an order conceptual thinking emerged from and pointed back to.

I considered an implication of appreciating the membership fallacy was that it meant that the world was innately self-ordered. And indeed worldly order was a prerequisite of reason. In a sort of transcendental argument, I said, if one asked 'Why?' and replied 'Because…', you could not accept the answer if it was possible that anything whatsoever could be the case, that your conclusion could be falsified. And this was what happened in a Chaos. Reason was founded on the premise that there was no chaos, that the world was ordered, so could not be employed to prove disorder. This was what in effect was attempted in the arguments that 'proved' the problem of induction.

The argument for innate order was an argument against the argument from design, which proved the existence of God. The latter was used to show that the order in the world required an Intelligent Designer; but I showed that order was logically necessary. The lack of creation showed the needlessness for a creator. And the ontological argument was refuted because things did not exist, even God, so could not necessarily exist. Kant said that all the reasons for the existence of God finally came to rest on the ontological argument. But that did not, in my mind, show that, though all the reasons for believing in God were refuted, we could only accept atheism. Spinoza, the rationalist philosopher, spoke of 'Deus sive Natura': 'God or Nature'. Why he used this proposition, I do not know; it may have been a definition in one of his proofs; though it is a weakness of Spinoza's method of argument that you don't have to accept the definitions. But if God was nature, and nature was descriptive, then God could be real. Indeed, God was Reality.

Again, if the world was a mathematical object, and the hurdles to reducing mathematics to logic represented by Russell's paradox and Godel's Theorem were removed, then the world was ultimately a logical object, and it was accessible to logical analysis. This was however only speculative.

Then finally, I brought together Relativity and Descriptivity, and could show how the latter reduced to the former, how Relativity explained Descriptivity.

I had for many years, compiled a manuscript book of my thoughts during each of the summer breaks whilst at Birkbeck. In 1992 I showed Paul Wolward, my friend at S.O.A.S, the thesis. I had rewritten it completely, from a literary point of view, that year, and had decided to exclude uncouth locutions, sentences that began 'It is...' or had the form 'The... of...'. I expressed my thoughts in simple words, short sentences and relatively short paragraphs. For my work avoided mystery or mock profundity, and it did not reduce the world to the human mind. Paul told me I should get it typed, which, after some months and with some difficulty, I managed to do. By the end of the year it was complete.

David Wiggins had examined the whole of the third chapter, the 'existential fallacy' I called it, which included the membership fallacy and my discoveries about existence. He made detailed criticisms and told me, to my surprise, that there were people who thought that things did not exist. They were called the 'predicativists'. Fiona had spoken of the 'quality of his mind'; that was one of the reasons she so admired him.

Then when my thesis was typed up, and David Wiggins had said it was beautifully written, I remembered something my father had said, all those years ago in Trinidad. He told me that when you submitted a manuscript for publication, it must be typed. Several times during my career I had said as I reached what I thought was a termination to my intellectual enterprise, 'Now I can die.' But I had discovered some new objection and consideration to my thoughts and for my mind to reflect on and solve. Now however, I felt I should get my typescript published. I had not formerly even conceived this.

When I graduated in 1993 it was with a good upper second. I had not done the reading and had forgotten how to study, though I missed none of the lectures. Scruton told me when he was my tutor in the second year that I could get a first. I told him I would not for just those reasons.

Other students had been speaking of 'when' they got their degrees; I had thought 'if' I got a degree. I honestly thought I might fail or get a third. But after the finals, an exam that was a 'federal' degree, the same papers being set for all the London colleges, and before I knew the result, I said that I had not done brilliantly, but I had not done too badly. When I got my degree I said to myself, 'Who would have thought the day would come?' After all those years of prison, epilepsy, mental home, insanity, homelessness and unemployment, I had done what others in my situation could not do. I had met several people, in the years of madness, who had been to university, even the best universities, and had their courses cut short by mental illness. Most had planned to go back; none would or could be imagined doing so. But I had. And that was not the end. I was aiming to get a book published. My ideas would not die with me.

In the years after graduation, I moved out of the council bed-sit I occupied for four or five years, and into another flat. But it was unsatisfactory. Something however happened at that time. Because I was an epileptic I was eligible for further social welfare benefits. These, taken with the others, meant that my income rose by a great degree. I was able to save money and go on a holiday to the continent, a thing I had not done since boyhood.

I got a private flat because, in a relatively short time I had amassed enough money to make the down payment. I had thousands of pounds in a bank account.

At the same time my intellectual enterprise met its zenith and I my nemesis. I started going to a strip-joint featuring young homosexual men and fell in love with a wild, working-class boy, a beautiful youth, who worked as a dancer and a prostitute. I was in awe of his virility, and was addicted to his company. I even took him back to my new home. But when I told him once I cared more for philosophy than sex, he howled. One day he said casually to me, in an off-hand way, 'I hope you get AIDS'. That was like him; he took and sold drugs and was casually cruel, out of control.

I got scared, for I had a terror of AIDS all through the eighties and was terrified now. I had been trying to publish my thesis for four years since graduation, but had not succeeded, or found the acceptances unacceptable. I now sent off the typescript to Cambridge University Press, who did not take me up, but with advice I took to heart about my book, told me to go to an independent academic publisher that they gave me the name and address of, saying they published good material. I sent it off to them and several months later, in 1997, my thesis was accepted for publication. Making some additions and alterations, my book was published under a different title from the one I had used all these years, but still of my choice; it was now called: 'The End of Existence.' That was in 1998.

I basked in the glory of my success, replete and content, with my intellectual enterprise becoming finally independent of myself and transcending me. But in the next year presage of my future personal destruction took place, in my being taken off all my psychotropic medication by an over-confident psychiatrist, and quickly having a nervous breakdown, something I avoided for over a decade, and being sectioned. Then in the following year, after a dispute involving payment for sexual favours, my author copies were stolen by the prostitute in the presence of his friends when I was absent from my flat. I overrated the disaster this was, but bought a knife and stabbed one of the friends of the prostitute who had been in the flat at the time.

He was wounded and I was charged with wounding with intent, a charge which led to a life sentence when taken with my previous offence of this kind, against the policeman, Ian Wheeler. That was in the year 2000. There are those who say that my book caused my downfall. I disagree. It was my salvation; it gave my life purpose, hope and meaning. The existentialists say that the world is absurd, but you can give your life meaning individually. That is not how I think, but they may have a point. And in intellectual terms, I .s succeeded. For the result of my thinking expressed in that book, far exceeded my original aims. The book was excellently written, and it was a triumph. I no longer control it, and my thoughts are known by academics on three continents. That is my vindication. That, and above all the intellectual achievement.

5. Past and Future
2006

Past

I did not do my philosophy to be published. It was not done for widespread fame, nor to gain wealth. In fact, I never earned a penny from it. I did not hope to become, in solving the intellectual difficulties, a holy man, or a great man, revered and respected. I did not become wise or good. The problems were solved despite the impediments to my progress in life. But it might be claimed they were solved because of those very 'hurdles', for I gained at least the leisure to apply myself to continuous thought. The impediments of prison, chronic epilepsy, mental home, mental illness released me from the ability or need to work.

The project was to solve an intellectual or logical problem, and that alone; for no gain other than that end. That was done to my satisfaction, and in excess of my expectations.

We are illogical creatures thrust into a complex, logical world. That is the absurdity of our condition. Accidents caused me to achieve my aim and to suffer the drawbacks. What can be learnt from this? Maybe we can understand the world: but can we understand ourselves? Or in understanding ourselves, we fail to factor in the world. Our predicament is absurd, yet the world is not. Holy men grasp, and even transcend, human nature; clever men grasp the world, a world that we may ultimately be only tiny parts of, and thereby redeem themselves from the incomprehensibility of selfhood and lose themselves in the total history, the developing universe.

Time, science tells us, is the fourth dimension of this world. There may be other worlds in other dimensions, with different physical laws. But metaphysics says what must hold in all possible worlds; and the study of it releases us from any particular universe and gives us knowledge of the mathematics of all worlds.

How must we feel when we are emancipated from the ties of time, world, dimension? Like a disembodied spirit. It is not our natural state, and we are not comfortable with it. Hume got it right: 'Be a philosopher, but in the midst of all your philosophy, still be a man'.

Remember the lines in the poem I wrote at the age of seventeen, before I started my quest? I spoke of the 'hollow knight' who found himself lost in the 'silent realms of Space'. The poem ends in lines I did not write at the start of this manuscript

> 'My place on Earth I have just found!
> Want nothing but the ground!'

Have I then spent my entire adult life journeying to comprehend something I dimly knew before I attempted the mission? That may be so. But I vaguely knew that things did not exist at the start of the enterprise. But it was knowing why that constituted the reason for going on. Knowing why gave me knowledge of the metaphysical world. Achieving this in the end gave me a quiet joy. That may in a sense outlive me: my body, mind, but it may be my eternal, disembodied spirit. It will not be, I hope, alone; it should join the ranks of the contributors to thought and be part of the living flow of ideas

My work is done and is free of me. I don't matter: my thought matters. I will suffer, grow old, and die. My ideas are pure and perfect. They continue to amaze me still in their perfection and my inability to correct them for the better.

I want now to reflect on the person and places these ideas were the children of. They did not come out of a study in an academy, surrounded by libraries and civilized, intelligent people. They came out of prisons, hostels for the disturbed, and sometimes conditions of real homelessness. The mind that produced them lived in the company of the poorly educated, was attacked by periods of mental breakdown and prolonged mental incapacity. It was not a gentle, decent mind, but managed to remain, in despite of everything, a logical mind, in love with concepts, and this love saved it from its destruction: long enough to complete the task it set itself.

All this goes to demonstrate that the academic mission is not solely achievable in the academy. Look: many of the great ideas were not produced by professionals working to earn a living by academic drudgery. It has only recently become the norm. So the worth of someone's thought is not to be evaluated by the mode of its presentation. Convention and conformity have deadened and laid waste the world of philosophy. It has become a job, a career; something done for the principal aim of gaining money. My father, back in Trinidad, said all you could do with philosophy was teach. I never felt that. The philosophy I was doing was to be produced originally. Can every thinker do this? Maybe not. But one should not say that the possibility of original thought, certainly in the present day, cannot arise.

Could I have done my work if I had become, as I determined in Keele at the age of nineteen, merely competent? If I had become, say, a teacher, and had not had the social and mental difficulties I subsequently encountered? I think not. My mind would have been lost in the complexities of scholarship, and I would have ended up concluding that 'the solution to the problem of induction is that it has no solution'. I would never have had the audacity to conceive of and maintain the existential fallacy and the membership fallacy. Too much that I had learnt would have to be unlearned, and whole systems and histories of thought that I grew up with in the academy would have to be abandoned. I would be left with no ground to stand on. Did Nature then pick the unlikeliest candidate to be the channel that millennia of civilized error was corrected through?

The value of the work is the only promise I now have that it will grow and thrive. But it must do that independently of myself, for, through the illogicality and irrationality of the self, I have fallen into the pit. Neither a good man nor a bad man would have attempted or achieved it. A man torn between both conditions was the vehicle for success. But now that the work is done it is plain that it was a benign obsession.

Future

My end draws near, but I do not look back on the past with longing, as some are wont to do. I recognise my coming demise, and that it may be in personal ignominy and darkness. I hope though that the product of my life survives even if my name does not, for it was always the content of the work that was my concern.

The world is of infinite complexity, but not chaotic. It may seem disordered; that though is only because we cannot discern the ultimate order. We may never be able to do this. I will disappear into time, and so will my lifetime's work. I will be forgotten; maybe however my intellectual contribution will influence other minds, other work, and finally and at last change the ways we think. That will be gradually.

I am glad my work is so succinct, so clear. This will help others who want to think along the same lines. It will of course, and I hope, be developed, and surely. I have got many things wrong; so change is in the offing. Not, though, by me. The point is that my life was useful, productive, even if I am unknown. I take pleasure in this. It is less than the great, but more than the mediocre. I was doomed to this by my nature, but I have been rescued from myself by my intellect and by circumstantial accidents. My life was more than most peoples' and less than a few.

Because I am locked into my subjectivity, I necessarily hope for ultimate achievement and recognition before I die. That is the same as hoping that one can live forever; but I do not believe this now. It is impossible however to be free of this irrational aspiration. The self cannot be free of awareness of selfhood. Not while life or consciousness persist. The self cannot imagine the lack of self, but the reason can. One should not, if one is not to be blown hither and thither by the forces of circumstance, surrender to the person. One cannot be purely rational, unfortunately.

Looking back on this narrative, I am struck by how humourless it seems. But my life was not so. My life is not what I recount; it is the unfolding of a philosophy through the life. That life was tragic, trivial, ridiculous, desperate, lost and found. Like some lives and unlike others. The pattern was not discerned until near the end; but the end has not yet arrived, and illumination and blackness inevitably await me.

Ingram Content Group UK Ltd.
Milton Keynes UK
UKHW020746120423
419992UK00002B/17